Sell Your Home Without Losing Your Zen

Diana Hathaway Timmons

Four Pines Press - 2008

Sell Your Home Without Losing Your Zen

By Diana Hathaway Timmons

First Published 2008

ISBN 978-0-6152-4078-7

Copyright © 2008 Diana Hathaway Timmons

All rights reserved. No part of this publication may be reproduced, stored in a retrieval system or transmitted in any form or by any means, electronic, mechanical or otherwise without the written permission of the Publisher.

Acknowledgements

Thank you to my family and friends who encourage me to dream big every day. You're the best.

Thank you to my clients who invite me into their homes, and lives, and make my work so very enjoyable.

Introduction

As I write this introduction for you, there are more than five million homes for sale in America. If you are one of the five million home sellers, I am happy to tell you that you hold in your hands the power to breeze through the stress of selling your home.

Sell Your Home Without Losing Your Zen is filled with a month of stories and meditations presented as an instruction manual, a good laugh, and a tonic for the most challenging days as a home seller. The process of selling your home won't change. You will. And that change will make all the difference in keeping your calm while your home is on the market.

This book was designed as a meditation-a-day to be read on a daily basis. If you like to jump right into a book, then reading it all in one sitting works too. You can then go back and read each day again. If you're like me, and love to peek at the end of the book first, you'll find the last chapter (and Day 31) is filled with helpful tips for selling your home.

So take a deep breath, find a comfy chair, and read on. Selling your home is about to get a lot more enjoyable.

1. Luck + Preparation = Success

One day, after weeks of waking up each morning and plunging into my cleaning routine in case the house would be shown, I decided to run to the bank before I was done. Leaving a stack of dirty dishes on the counter, I rationalized to myself, "who would want to show my house on a Wednesday morning?" I just needed to get out.

After visiting the bank, I decided that as it was such a beautiful morning, I'd take a walk by the harbor. It was just a short walk. As I returned to my car, my cell phone rang. It was a terrible connection, but I could glean that a real estate agent wanted to show my house. However, he wanted to show it NOW. He was down the street from my house with clients in the car. I had to delay the showing, as I knew there was a stack of dirty dishes on the counter. I asked for 10 minutes to get home and tend to the dishes. The real estate agent agreed.

As I ran through my foyer, after racing down the local streets, the real estate agent called back to say that his clients did not want to wait, and perhaps he'd try to bring them back tomorrow. I tortured myself the rest of the afternoon and evening over it. The real estate agent did call back the next day, and the house was shown in its proper condition.

Today...

    I will do everything in my power to make it easy for real estate agents and buyers to see my home. If I truly cannot look at another dust bunny or dirty dish, I will head to the beach, but only if I can do this without punishing myself for it if the call does come. Otherwise, I will be sitting with my toes in the sand, not enjoying it, but feeling guilt and panic over what may happen while I'm gone.

2. Details

I have noticed, as my house is on the market, that I have become obsessed with the tiniest details: a speck of dust on the dresser, a fingerprint on the mirror, a small weed popping up on the driveway. This attention to detail serves me well as the house should reflect that level of care. I can also take this too far. Asking my family members to walk on the outside edges of the carpeted stairs to avoid making imprints is asking too much, apparently. I am learning to balance my vision of a perfect house, and the needs of those that live here with me.

Today...

    I will respect the boundaries of others while my house is for sale. While my neighbor's driveway may have a small weed growing in the crack, I will resist the temptation to pull it up for them.

3. Flyers

In my city right now there are many homes for sale. Some homes for sale have high-quality, color flyers available at the signpost, two have black and white cheaply made flyers, and two have no flyers available. Some flyer boxes are full, and many are perpetually empty.

Color flyers are expensive to produce, but are so helpful in selling your home. The home seller is often asked to maintain the flyer boxes. It's a great use of your time. Do not become so obsessed, as perhaps I have been, to count the flyers each day to see what has been taken.

Today...

    I will be sure that anyone driving by my house has a good-quality, dry, typo-free flyer available to them. I will respect my neighbor's flyers and resist the temptation to take one of their flyers, "just to see what it's listed for," then toss it in the trash at home. I will also educate my children in flyer etiquette the first time they come home with a stack of them from the neighbor's yard, and begin to color on them.

4. Clutter

When prospective buyers enter your home, you want to convey a feeling that living in this home will be carefree. Though my family laughs at me, I am adamant about keeping toilet paper rolls full. The typical items in the medicine cabinet are cleverly positioned out of sight. My storage containers in the kitchen are sitting in a simple basket, perfectly organized.

When a buyer looks at my home, they believe in their hearts that no one in this house has headaches, runs out of toilet paper, or ever spends a minute scouring the cabinets for a lid that fits a storage container. My closet is organized by color, and I've used all one color plastic hangers. I love living this way, and vow to myself to keep this up once we move into a new home.

This is not false advertising of a lifestyle that does not exist in this home, but instead a result of consciously living in a clutter-free environment that allows me to enjoy the home even more.

Today...

    I will remember as I prepare my home for sale, that what I do to make my home enticing for buyers, I can do for myself now, and in the future. I will use my best china, burn the prettiest candles, and organize my home so that living here really is carefree. I will love the new routines and vow to embrace them in my new home. I will learn to enjoy the process of making my home beautiful, not just for buyers but also for myself.

5. Graciousness

Being a gracious home seller not only improves your chances of selling more quickly, it can also make your life more peaceful. Being around the real estate business, I have heard the horror stories of sellers who, though needing to sell their house, have berated real estate agents and buyers who dared inconvenience them while it is on the market.

I welcome all real estate agents who would like to show my home. I make it easy for them in every way possible. If it means I race home with minutes to spare to make sure my home looks perfect, I'll do that with no complaint. If I'm caught off-guard, real estate agents and buyers are met with a smile, a welcoming word, and my quick exit. If you would like to sell your home, accommodation must become your middle name. It can be inconvenient, unfair, and even irritating, but it's necessary.

If your home earns a reputation for being hard to show and as an uncooperative seller, you've made it even harder to sell your home. Being gracious even in the face of the disruption of having your home on the market reaps benefits to your own inner peace. Why create adversaries when there are none?

Today...

    I will remind myself daily that I have a product for sale. I will live in the awareness that real Estate is a people business above all. I will imagine how it would feel to enter an unfamiliar little store, and be turned away or treated badly by the shopkeeper. Would it make me feel good about the store? Would I purchase anything there? I have the power to make the home sale experience whatever I choose.

6. Pride

I recently read a great blog written by a real estate pro. He said that the minute you have an amount in your mind that you have to get out of your home when it sells, you're sunk. You're counting on money you don't have, and it could be keeping you from seeing your home and the market realistically. His words really hit home.

I realized that the notion of what I expected to get from my home was causing me to ignore the reality of the market and not make the soundest decisions in evaluating offers. I think it's natural to overvalue that which is dear to us, but buyers will not be buying our special memories of the house. Our pride can keep us from seeing our home clearly.

Today...

I will remember that the happy memories of this home will travel with me when I move out. When I acknowledge that when my emotional connection is removed from my home, the value becomes what buyers will pay for it. I won't let pride stand in my way of selling my home and moving on to another special connection with my new home.

7. Waiting

It isn't easy to wait for a buyer. If you're selling in a buyer's market, you can second-guess every detail of your home, your marketing, and your very worth. As I wait for buyers, it's the lack of control of the situation that can stress me out. You may find that the act of preparing your home each day for a possible showing, attending to each detail in the house, staying on top of the market, gives you some sense of control that is glaringly lacking in waiting for buyers to see your home.

I find that vacuuming is my weapon of choice to combat the waiting nerves. If your home is priced realistically, if you have confidence in your agent, if you've done your homework, then no amount of cajoling or nagging your agent will sell the house. It will only stress both of you out.

Today…

     I will accept that waiting is part of this dance. I may get a showing tomorrow. I may get a showing in two weeks. Once I have prepared my home, and tapped into my graciousness, I can only wait. I have confidence in my home and in my real estate agent. If not, I will make the necessary changes to gain that confidence so that I can relax and allow the process to happen. I will empty the vacuum canister regularly so that it's available to me 24/7 when all else fails.

8. Wabi Sabi

Wabi Sabi: The art of imperfection. In my quest for total perfection in my home for sale, it's easy to go overboard. I've heard the questions from buyers and agents asking if anyone actually lives in my house. While I am going for that model home experience, I can't lose sight that a house can be *too* perfect. We want buyers to feel comfortable and see themselves living in the home, not be afraid to touch anything for fear of disrupting the displays.

I try to strike a balance between a beautiful product for sale, and something a buyer can live with. The Japanese call this Wabi Sabi: the art of imperfection. Inside my perfectly prepared home you might find a tired throw tossed over the corner of a lovely sofa, a cat toy peering out from under a chair, a smudge on the bathroom mirror.

Today…

I will remember that this is a home for people, not a magazine photo shoot. I will strive to make my home beautiful, clean, and appealing to buyers, yet embrace imperfection. I will never, ever, use Wabi Sabi as an excuse to get out of doing the dishes.

9. Obsession

Perhaps it was my Mother's exasperated tone when she asked "are we ever going to talk about anything besides real estate?" I suddenly realized that I had hit a point in my life when selling my house became all-consuming. I would go to sleep thinking about the house. I'd wake up thinking about the house. I looked at the emails I'd been sending out recently, and the subject of selling the house dominated all other subjects at an alarming rate.

While I think there is value in putting your best effort in preparing your house for sale, and becoming a knowledgeable seller, apparently you can go too far. I had become a bore.

Today...

    I will accept that the selling of my home is not as fascinating to everyone as it is to me, and hopefully my real estate agent. While I may receive polite inquiries about my progress, it doesn't require more than a simple update. Though my life may be on a roller coaster right now, there is no need to fill the other cars with loved ones, friends, neighbors, people in line at the grocery store, and anyone within earshot. I will buy a journal early on in the selling process, and fill it daily.

10 signs you've become obsessed with selling your home:

Your friends avoid you.
Your neighbors avoid you.
Your real estate agent avoids you.
You have a bumper sticker that reads: Ask me about my house.
You count the flyers every morning to see if any are missing.
You've buried 300 St. Joseph statues in your yard.
You've stopped cooking altogether so the kitchen will stay clean.
You can calculate the price per square foot of any home without a calculator.
You've figured out how to get down the stairs without leaving footprints in the carpet.
You received 50 copies of this book for your birthday.

10. Crowd Pleaser

There is a hard lesson in selling your home that doesn't come without some discomfort. The lesson is that you cannot be all things to all buyers. Your house will not appeal to everyone. Every time you think you've figured things out, they will change. You'll have five buyers say that your lack of stainless steel appliances keeps them from making an offer, so you outfit the home with new stainless appliances. Then the next five buyers say that your yard isn't right for them.

You can prepare your home beautifully, price your home right, and do everything right. You do all those things and yet you still have to wait for the buyer that wants the exact combination of price, location, and feeling that your home conveys. There is no way around this. You cannot please every buyer, but you shouldn't despair. If you carefully prepare your home, your home can appeal to a wider audience.

Today...

I will prepare my home to the best of my ability, and listen to honest feedback with an open mind. My goal is to avoid anything that would immediately put my house out of contention with similar homes. I will accept that I cannot please all buyers, but will strive to be attractive to the largest audience possible. I will not take the feedback personally.

11. Optimism

Sometimes it's hard to stay positive if your home has been on the market a while. I would be lying if I wrote that I have always stayed positive while I was selling a home. Even if the home had offers in the first week, I could always find things to feel negative about, like knowing an offer is coming, but assuming it'll be a low offer and finding myself worked into a cycle of negativity. What we tell ourselves as home sellers can make either the experience a nightmare or a dream. Okay, maybe dream is overstating it a bit. Let's just say it can be mostly positive or negative based upon how we view it.

For me, optimism keeps it a mostly positive experience. When that doubt and negativity creep in I tell myself that at any moment the phone could ring and a showing or even an offer might be hours away. I remind myself that at every minute someone out there is making life decisions that may include buying my house. Assuming the worst doesn't make it an easier wait. It makes it harder. If I really need to let out the negative thoughts, I'll allow myself a short and melodramatic episode in which I can rant and cry and blame everyone but myself. I will set a timer for five minutes for my little drama, then wash my face, fluff the pillows, and get over it.

Today...

    I will catch myself when I hear pessimistic thoughts running through my mind. I will replace them with an understanding that I can't know the rhythm of the world, and at any moment everything can change. I trust that I've done everything I can to prepare my house, and can choose to wait patiently or miserably.

12. Practice Makes Perfect

Doing the same thing over and over again and expecting a different result is a definition of insanity. It is also called getting your house ready for showing each morning before you leave for work. The little rituals you adopt while selling a home may get tiresome after weeks or months on the market. There is nothing wrong with your rituals. While doing the same thing over and over and expecting a different result may seem insane, it is also a characteristic of the greatest athletes and constant achievers.

Today...

I will continue my daily routine of making my home attractive to buyers. There will be many mornings where I will doubt myself, and even be tempted to skip this ritual. I will not be tempted. I will understand that performing these chores, though repetitious, will one day sell my home.

13. The Enemy Within

As my house sat on the market for over a month, I considered a price change but rejected it each time. I knew that the market simply lacked buyers. I was confident my home was priced right and nicely presented. A challenge for me was that the two houses nearby were also for sale. One afternoon I received a call from my real estate agent. She sounded grave. She told me that my neighbor had just slashed her asking price by $20,000. Her home, slightly larger than mine with more luxurious features, was now priced less than mine.

I was upset all afternoon. I shared my indignation with my husband, my mother, my sister, and anyone I could reach. The next day I thought again about the price change. I reminded myself that she did not do this to spite me. They did this because they desperately wanted to sell their home. Once I turned my thinking around, I became peaceful with the change. Would it make things harder for me? Absolutely. Did they make that change to be malicious? Absolutely not.

Today...

    I will believe the best in others, especially when I'm offering my home for sale. It does me no good to create enemies where there are none. I will treat people fairly, give them the benefit of the doubt, and will stop trying to read minds. I will price my home based upon research, advice from professionals, and my own intuition. I will not get caught up in fear-based competitive price-lowering with the neighbors.

14. Rejection

There comes a point in every home selling venture when rejection rears its ugly head. You may sell your home in days, and yet there are the comments relayed from the buyer regarding your color choice, carpet, approach to housekeeping. Or you could experience the greatest rejection: Teetering on the edge of an offer but losing out to another home. In a buyer's market, this scenario plays out daily for sellers around the world. The rejection may be different, it may be small or large, but it feels the same.

I vowed to take a Buddha like approach the last time I sold my home, and my cool facade remained fairly unscathed. I did, however, break out in a fierce rash instead. I realized that cool facades really impress those around you, but if you're feeling rejected or stressed, it's okay to experience it. By fully experiencing your disappointment, you allow yourself to move past it naturally, and move toward optimism.

Today...

    I will stop trying to manage my disappointment. I will allow myself to feel badly when things don't go my way. Putting a brave and positive face to the world is a goal, but I will not sacrifice my inner peace by playacting. I will not bore others with stories of every slight and every setback, but will be willing to share that I am hurting sometimes. Then, I'll move past it, and expect good news soon.

15. Because Nice matters

There will be times while in a real estate transaction you'll be involved with people who are, well, not nice people. Humans are by nature helpful and nice. You may be stunned by the actions of buyers and potential buyers because we naturally expect pleasant cooperation from strangers. As we waited for a buyer we were tormented by the behavior of one set of prospective buyers. We got mixed messages, maybes, mights, and then rejection. We tried to understand their behavior, but when it was clear that they were truly not nice people, we gave up.

It is impossible to understand bizarre, rude, or greedy, behavior if you are none of these yourself.

Today...

    I will remember that the world is full of all types of people with their own agendas. I will not torture myself trying to understand the behaviors of someone that does not share my beliefs on how we treat others. The Golden Rule only applies to myself, as I'm the only person I can control. I will learn to let go of expectations.

16. Under the Sink

Have you looked under your sink lately? When preparing my home for sale, the areas beneath all sinks are given a thorough makeover. Yes, people do open those cabinets beneath the sink. This is something the men usually do. They look at the pipes. It's like kicking the tires on a car. Even if your pipe hasn't leaked in all the time you've owned this house, a disheveled cabinet will make a buyer believe otherwise.

I remove everything that is not crucial under the sinks. I make sure the assorted bottles and supplies are in good condition. Always clean inside the cabinet thoroughly, so that a leaking bottle is not confused for a leaking pipe.

Today...

I will remember to look beneath the surface. To buyers, what goes on under my sink is as important as what goes on in the sink. I will take that knowing into every room of the house, making every cabinet and drawer pleasing to inquisitive buyers. Beauty is more than skin deep.

17. Pets

I love my pets. For many homeowners, the pets are part of the family. That part of the family does complicate selling your home. Cats have litter boxes. Do you hide it away for all showings? Do you stash the box and the cat each time you leave the house just in case? Because I believe that there may be many buyers that either don't like cats or are allergic, I take the time to sequester the kitty to the garage along with his cat box when I leave the house. Buyers may know intellectually that you own a cat, but seeing the cat box conjures up every negative feeling they may have about them, and suddenly they are sure they can smell the cat.

What about the dogs? Do you leave them in the backyard during showings? I think that they distract, and their barking hastens people to move through the house faster than they usually would. When I have advance notice of a showing, the pets take a ride with me, after I have tucked away all of their accessories in my home. If I must leave without the pets, they stay in the garage with a nice note on the door alerting the real estate agent and buyers that pets are in the garage. I offer my cell phone number if they have any questions or problems. This has worked beautifully for the impromptu showings that have happened while I was away.

Today...

I will make it easy for buyers to love my home, whether they love pets or not. I will understand that not everyone loves cats or dogs as much as I do. I will work to make this experience less stressful on the pets, as well, making sure they are comfortably accommodated during their exile.

18. The Garage

I had not given much thought about our garage as I prepared the house for sale. It became a place for boxes I'd already packed, miscellaneous things that didn't fit anywhere else, and general clutter. Because the pets were left in there during some showings, I'd put the garage out of my mind. And yet, the condition of the garage gnawed at me. I knew that it had to be dealt with. I know that most of us don't want to deal with our garages. They have become a last stop for clutter that needs to go somewhere else. When I finally faced the fact that I had to make the garage presentable, I researched home buyer's preferences.

Not surprising, the garage is a major consideration for male home buyers. As wonderful as my home looked on the inside, I was neglecting something so important to buyers. The garage. While the home was on the market we'd hear from real estate agents that the wife loved the home, but the husband preferred something else. Once I tackled the garage, cleaning it out so well that two cars could actually park in there, our husband/wife equation equalized.

Today...

    I will not forget that the garage is as important that the house, and the yard. I will rent a storage unit if I must, to remove the clutter that is holding my garage back. I will revel in the fact that my home is now a complete and perfect package. And, I will enjoy parking in my garage once again.

19. Persistence

As I write this, my home has been on the market for a while. This is a slow market of historical proportions. Because I understand this, I'm able to weather it fairly well. I am, however, human. I have my moments of frustration, where I silently yell at the cars that stop to take a flyer, "Please! Please! Buy my house!" Mostly, I wake up each morning and repeat my routine that readies the house for showing, knowing that this day could be the day.

Sadly, I witnessed a home seller who had gone over the edge. While tending to my flyer box near the entrance to my neighborhood, a car drove up alongside me. He asked if I was looking to buy a home. I told him I had one for sale. Disappointed, he told me that he had a house for sale in a nearby neighborhood and when he saw me taking a flyer he'd decided to pull over and tell me about his house. There is persistence, and then there is desperation.

Today...

    I will persist in the routines that make my home ready for a buyer to see. I know that persistence pays off eventually. It may be hard to keep the faith when I feel as though I've done this a thousand times, but deep in my soul I know that my turn is coming. I will neither resort to actually yelling at passing cars, nor stop people on the street to tell them about my house.

20. 100 Blind Dates

This morning, as I was preparing the house for the day, I laughed to myself thinking that selling my home felt like having 100 blind dates. I know nothing about the buyers who will be coming into my home, scrutinizing my lifestyle, and critiquing my home's appearance. I know that they will bring their own needs, experiences, and biases to the occasion. Like a blind date, I strive to present my home's best qualities, without knowing what will capture my buyer's heart.

I know that real estate, like love, can be blind. My home may answer every specific need for a particular buyer, yet the offer doesn't arrive. And like love, another buyer for whom my house does not particularly work, might very well make an offer because they just knew it was "the one".

Today...

     I will remember that like a blind date, my home cannot be all things to all buyers. I will remember that real estate is an emotional business, and every buyer brings with them their own baggage. I know in my heart that choosing a home is like choosing a life partner. It's not the specific features that make us fall in love, but just the right combination. Like in love, I will strive to remove the deal-breakers that disqualify my home from courtship with my buyers. I know that eventually my Prince or Princess Charming will arrive and will live happily ever after in my home.

21. Keeping it Fresh

If your home has been on the market for some time, it's easy to rest on your laurels. We have our established routines each morning to have the house ready for the day. We spend a Saturday morning doing more in-depth cleaning. After that first rush of putting the house on the market and preparing for the broker's open house, the house settles into a comfortable routine. If your house is on the market more than a month, you'll want to add something to your routine.

Every 3 or 4 weeks evaluate the condition of your home. Are the flowers on your front porch starting to look tired? Do your flowerbeds need weeding again? Has dust or cobwebs settled anywhere? Do the light switches need a quick wipe again? When we see things daily we begin to no longer notice them. A house that was freshly staged for sale 4 weeks ago will now be showing some signs of tiredness.

Today...

I will re-evaluate my home with a fresh eye every few weeks. I know that I can become used to even the most perfectly presented home, and not see the smudges, dying flowers, or pet fur. Just as a retail store shifts their merchandise around on a regular basis, I will remember that I too am selling a product, and will keep it fresh.

10 Little Indulgences For Your Home:

Fresh flowers – Buy only a bouquet you love.
Fabulous new Dish towels that make you happy.
Scented reed oil diffuser - Great for a subtle scent.
Make or buy a seasonal wreath for your front door.
A few gorgeous magazines for your coffee table.
A bath at the groomer for your pet.
An artisan doorbell.
Hanging flower baskets for your yard.
A beautiful bowl of fruit for your kitchen.
A luxurious throw for your favorite chair.

22. Holidays

My home was on the market as we approached the Christmas holidays. As a seller, this presents problems and opportunities. Many home sellers pull their house off the market between Thanksgiving and late January. Those sellers believe that few buyers will be shopping around the holidays, or the sellers want to enjoy the holidays without the stress of having their home on the market.

I chose to leave the house on the market through the holidays. I knew that if buyers were to materialize at that time, they would be serious buyers. Because so many other sellers pulled their homes off the market at that time, my home would have less competition. Also, I believed that a home beautifully decorated for the holidays would go a long way to make a buyer fall in love.

For my Christmas decorating, I brought out one third of our usual decorations. Enough to make the house feel decorated, but not so much as to make a buyer feel they had walked in on a stranger's Christmas celebration.

Today…

I will not assume that my home should disappear over the holidays. There are all kinds of life transitions that create a buyer at any time of the year. I will honor my family's holiday traditions, but make sure my potential visitors feel right at home.

23. The Domino Effect

As I wait for the right buyer to walk through my door, and that solid offer to follow, I have already peeked at many potential replacement homes. Though I'm not ready to make an offer, it gives me inspiration to vacuum the floors every day, and live this lifestyle to get the house sold. I have had favorites that I check out online from time to time. I watch their price reductions, I critique their photos, and sometimes I watch them disappear from the MLS. Then, I find new homes to watch, waiting for my turn to buy.

One day I realized that just as I'm watching homes I'd like to buy when my house sells; then buyers are likely watching MY house while they wait for their house to sell. Real estate thrives on the Domino Effect.

Today...

I will enjoy my little indulgence of tracking homes I might want to buy. I'll take solace in knowing that somewhere out there buyers are watching my house, too. When the dominoes start to fall in my direction, I'll be ready.

24. Curb Appeal

Half the battle in selling your home is getting the buyers past the front door. Buyers will drive by your house at least once before deciding to tour inside. Even buyers from out of the area, who find your house online, will often drive by the day before an appointment to meet with their real estate agent and tour homes. Your house needs to be irresistible from the curb.

Each morning I wake up and pull the front blinds, turn on the lights in the front of the house, and give the house a welcoming look. Until bedtime, I keep the lights on in the front of the house, and the blinds pulled up. I've had to duck out of sight many times during the evening, as potential buyers pull up in front of the house to take a flyer and witness the curb appeal. I've gotten very good at darting out of sight, though a few potential buyers have actually waved at me.

Today…

    I will remember that buyers will judge this book by its cover. I will keep the porch welcoming and uncluttered. My porch lights will be functional and on during the evenings. I will convey a sense of warmth and comfort from the curbside view. I want to give buyers passing by the impression that the best is yet to come.

25. Forensic Vacuuming

Selling your home doesn't have to be all work and no fun. The cleverest home sellers find amusing ways to break up the monotony of preparing the house for sale each day. In my home, I have perfected the art of what I call "forensic vacuuming". If I have the luxury of time before a showing, I completely vacuum the house. It not only looks fabulous, it can yield clues as to the success of your showing.

Upon returning home after the showing I go through each room analyzing the footprints. Did they look out the windows? Did they walk all the way into the room or was it a precursory glance from the doorway? Did they open closets? Did they sit in the living room? By analyzing the footprint patterns I can usually deduce how serious those buyers were with amazing accuracy. Obsessive? Silly? Perhaps. But it sure makes the waiting more interesting, and gives your real estate agent something to laugh about.

Today...

I will remember that selling my home doesn't have to be all work and no play. Though I may be stressed or tired, I will try to find the humor in every situation, even if I appear very, very, foolish to my real estate agent.

26. The Power of Cookies

Scientific evidence now shows that we fall in love using all our senses. When we sell our homes, we're asking buyers to fall in love with our homes. I swear by the power of cookies. There is nothing like the scent of vanilla and cinnamon to make your buyers feel at home.

I keep a package of slice and bake cookie dough in my refrigerator. Shortly before a showing I bake a batch of cookies, sprinkled liberally with cinnamon. The cookies are placed on a nice plate, with a homemade note asking buyers to "enjoy the cookies while you tour our home." I add a stack of colorful napkins, and a few bottles of water.

I have received countless comments that the cookies were a "wonderful touch". Better yet, every time I've baked those cookies our house has placed in the top 3 choices for that those buyers.

Today...

I will know that the way to a buyer's heart is through their stomachs. The act of baking cookies and setting a place for my potential buyers is my way of welcoming them into my home like honored guests. I will resist the temptation to count the cookies and spiral downward into forensic baking.

27. Sometimes It Rains

If you happen to be selling in a buyer's market, it's hard to avoid the doom and gloom in the media and online. The frightening stories are everywhere you turn: Buyers making spectacularly low offers, of home builders offering incentives like new cars and vacations, and buyers making multiple offers on the same day to see which will accept at the lower price.

You can't live in a bubble and avoid hearing this tales. Nor can you avoid compelling statistics that tell you that you're selling in a buyer's market. Your only defense in that environment is confidence and realism. If you're working with a real estate agent sit down with them and pore over the numbers for your area regularly. Watch the market trends to be sure your home continues to be priced correctly.

Don't be so set on a price that you miss opportunities to sell your house, but don't be too eager to accept that price is the only factor if your house is not selling right away.

Today...

It's okay to feel angry, nervous, or even hopeless, at times when faced with the prospect of lowering your price yet again, or accepting an offer that doesn't allow you to move forward with your life plans. Don't let those emotions stop you from doing what needs to be done to sell your home. If you can fix what is keeping your house on the market, then fix it. If not, practice acceptance.

A great Buddhist sage said it best: If something can be fixed, why worry? If something cannot be fixed, why worry?

10 things you can do right now to grab some Zen:

Go outside and check on your landscaping.
Go outside and check on your flyer supply.
Write a love letter to your house.
Grab color markers and make a "cookie" sign.
Take photos of your landscaping.
Give your dog a bath
Take a long hot bath.
Bake cookies for yourself.
Take a drive to look at model homes.
Call a friend and talk about something other than your house.

28. Photo Finish

I stumbled across an online debate between real estate agents about the practice of removing all family photos from a home before putting it on the market. You may have heard that having photos in your house prevents a buyer from imagining themselves living in your home. No photos can make a house feel empty or sterile. A wall of photos will distract buyers, as we're naturally curious for hints of who lives in the house.

I come down somewhere in the middle of the argument. A few nice photos grouped on a piano or dresser looks homey and natural. Using similar or matching frames really unifies a group of photos. Avoid elaborate displays, as they will only distract.

One home that I toured used photos in a stunning way. The homeowner purchased a digital photo frame, the kind that rotates a series of photos. They set the frame upon a table in the living room. Each photo features aspects of the home like the sunset view, the garden, the house during the holidays, etc. It was a brilliant idea for using photos in your home. I plan to recommend this to my clients.

Today...

    I will edit my photos to show off my home's features, not my family. The photos I'll display will be attractively framed, meaningful, and few. When I get to my new home, I'll give my family photos a place of honor again.

29. Generosity

One couple considering an offer on my home, were also expecting a new baby at any minute. Moved by their situation, I purchased the loveliest yarn for a baby, and crocheted a hat for their soon-to-be newborn. I knew that an offer was not guaranteed, but it felt nice to do something while I waited. The buyers purchased another home immediately after their daughter's birth. I dropped the baby gift off at their agent's office with a card, and an explanation to the agent.

Often, when a serious buyer emerges, I'm alert for clues about them. If a potential buyer is moving in from out of town, I imagine putting together a basket of books and brochures about our area. If the buyer is a gardener, I think of ways to let them know about the plants in the garden. I plan to let my neighbors know about the new homeowners so that introductions will be made, and they'll feel at home right away.

Today...

    I will explore ways to be generous, even though this is a time when I also hope to receive. I will strive to give in ways that will personalize the sale of my home, and provide comfort to others during this stressful time. I will never forget that there are people on either side of the transaction.

30. Victory

The day has finally arrived. You have accepted an offer, passed the home inspection, waited through the long days of escrow, and the deal is done. You have navigated the emotional waters of selling your home. You have survived the ups and downs of indecisive buyers, low offers, and stacks of paperwork.

Congratulations!

Today…

I vow that I will never sell my house again.

Well, maybe I'll just vow that next time I'll be better prepared, thicker-skinned, and even more Zen. I know that I will sell another house eventually, and I will approach it with the same wide-eyed optimism that this time will be different.

I will keep this book handy.

31. Practical Matters

Inspiration is wonderful, but practicality rules. In the course of selling my own homes, and preparing client's homes for sale, I've picked up many great tips and resources. Here are my favorites that may help you navigate the process, and even make your life easier.

What about those shoes? Keep a boot tray inside the front door. I found a beautiful and reasonably priced metal boot tray that I've set inside the front door. Buyers touring your home may take that as a cue to remove their shoes. This not only keeps your floors clean, but also suggests to the buyers that your floors are in good shape because you don't wear outside shoes in the house.

Welcome. Be sure your doormat is fresh and up-to-date with the season. Watch for fraying on the coir mats, as they can track little bits of material into your house. An all-season mat in a durable material works best.

Scents. I favor cinnamon and vanilla in scenting my home for sale. There are many reed diffusers, or plug in fresheners, available with the yummy scents that buyers love. A clean laundry scent is also a hit with buyers. Be careful of over-scenting your home with plug-ins. Have a friend, or your real estate agent, come over and promise to be honest about the scent condition of your home, especially if you have pets.

Cooking. Under no circumstances should you let anyone convince you that it would be okay to cook bacon, curry chicken, or fish, if you think that the following day or two might yield a showing. Don't cave on this issue. Trust me.

Toilet paper. Yes, I'm really writing a tip about toilet paper. When you're selling your home, the roll end should face in toward the holder, as in "over" the roll, so there is no tail. Perhaps this tip will finally settle those "over" vs. "under" battles in your home.

Baskets. I'm a big fan of baskets in organizing your house, with a caveat: The baskets should be square, non-cutesy, made with natural materials, and they should be used sparingly. They are great for organizing storage containers, trash bags, paper plates, and other loose items in the kitchen. I put large and sturdy baskets in the closets to contain kid shoes, toys, or books. I use baskets in the pantry to corral small items.

Vacuuming. I'm sure you've gathered by now that vacuuming is a major component of having a showing-ready home. There is a chance I've become obsessed with it, but with relatively little effort you can keep even an aging carpet looking fresh. The alternative is replacing the carpeting or giving an allowance to your buyers. I think a good vacuuming routine is preferable.

Vacuuming: the Sequel. I have just discovered the beauty of adding an additional weapon in your floor care arsenal. I've purchased a lightweight, battery-operated sweeper. The sweeper charges up and runs for about an hour per charge. It's great for quick touch ups when you don't want to drag out the vacuum. Most work on both bare floors and medium to lower pile carpets. My sweeper flattens out to move under furniture, and the pole is removable to make stairs a breeze.

www.ingramcontent.com/pod-product-compliance
Lightning Source LLC
Chambersburg PA
CBHW051714040426
42446CB00008B/885